ANIMALS in CROSS-STITCH

ANNIEN TEUBES

δελος
Cape Town

ACKNOWLEDGEMENTS

1 My family that constantly encouraged me and criticized where necessary.
2 Màrike Smit for all her help with the embroidery for the photographs.
3 D.M.C.
4 Da Vinci Picture Framers, Durbanville.

CONTENTS

Foreword   3
Materials   3
Embroidery thread   3
Needles   3
Frames   3
Scissors   4
General hints   4
French knot   4
 1 Rabbit   6
 2 Tiger   9
 3 Frog   11
 4 Squirrel   13
 5 Parrot   14
 6 Duck   17
 7 Ostrich   19
 8 Butterfly   21
 9 Tortoise   22
10 Giraffe   25
11 Zebra   26
12 Lion   29
13 Hippopotamus   30
14 Kittens   32

© 1989 Delos Publishers, 40 Heerengracht, Cape Town

All rights reserved. No part of this book may be reproduced or transmitted in any form or by any means, electronic or mechanical, including photocopying, recording or by any information storage and retrieval system, without the written permission of the publisher.
Photography by Bart Steyn
Styling by Mandi Smit
Translation by Maria Kerbelker
Cover design by Abie and Jasmine Fakier
Set in 11 on 12 pt Helvetica
Printed and bound by National Book Printers, Goodwood, Cape
First edition 1989

ISBN 1 86826 042 9

FOREWORD

Our lives are very rushed, and at the end of a long day we find that more often than not, we are intensely frustrated, because we have not achieved anything.
Join me now and discover the delight of cross-stitch, one of the easiest ways of getting rid of all the accumulated tension.
Take your embroidery with you and use every stolen moment to create something beautiful.
BRIEFLY something about the history of cross-stitch: Cross-stitch is one of the types of embroidery found almost everywhere on earth. In Europe it is found in the early "Peasant embroidery", where predominantly big designs and red and black threads were used.
During the Victorian era many a young lady embroidered a fine sampler with information about her or her family. Letters and figures were used, as well as patterns of little animals, flowers, birds, houses and even human figures.
Nowadays, "Cottage style" and very modern designs are used for cross-stitch. Basically any pattern with the correct setting and frame can, however, be adapted to fit in with the rest of the decor.
Let us now look at a few general guidelines before we begin to embroider.

MATERIALS

Today cross-stitch material comes in prepackaged, ready-cut sizes and also in varying density. This makes embroidery even easier.
You may, however, use any even-weave, hardanger or Aïda cloth. These fabrics are available in a variety of colours and thread density.
The thread density, usually over 2,5 cm, will in other words determine the size of your end product. In this book a fourteen-count fabric is mainly used. Should you thus use an eleven-count fabric, your finished article will be bigger. The reason for this is simple: there are fewer stitches on the same area.

EMBROIDERY THREAD

D.M.C. stranded embroidery thread is used throughout. The number of strands is normally determined by the thread-count of your fabric, but your embroidery tension and the colour of the fabric can also have an influence. (Dark colours are inclined to show through and therefore require more thread.)
The following table is usually a good guideline, but test your embroidery tension and adapt the number of threads accordingly.

Number of stitches per 2,5 cm	Number of threads
11	3
14	2 or 3
18	2
22	1 or 2

When you cut thread lengths, remember to always keep the colour codes and do not cut the embroidery thread into sections that are too long. (45 cm is a good length.) If more than one strand of a specific colour is needed, buy them all together and make sure they have precisely the same colour code, as they may differ slightly from consignment to consignment. Keep scraps together with their numbers so that they could later be used, because sometimes only a few stitches are done in a particular colour.

NEEDLES

Blunt-pointed tapestry needles are used for cross-stitch. The needle size will be determined by the thread count of your fabric. Use a thicker needle for a coarser fabric. All the needles, however, have a large eye with a fine point. A number 24 needle is usually suitable, except for very fine fabrics, where a finer needle should be used.

FRAMES

Embroidery hoops are available in different sizes. Acquire a good one suitable for your requirements.

SCISSORS

A small pair of sharp-pointed scissors is an essential part of your equipment. Threads must be evenly trimmed.

GENERAL HINTS

Determine the size of your project and cut the fabric 4 cm wider around the edges. This is very important for the mounting, finishing or frame of your picture.
Immediately finish all raw edges with a zigzag stitch or if you do not have a machine, put masking tape right around to prevent the edges from fraying.
Find the centre of the fabric. Gently fold the material in half in order to determine the centre of the sides. Use a needle and ordinary machine cotton and sew a tacking stitch over each cross-stitch sized square across the length of the material.
Do the same with the width, but start in the middle and work towards the edges. The intersection of the vertical and horizontal lines is the centre point. Determine the centre point on the graph. This is where you start your embroidery.
Ensure that your hands are clean before you start, as the end result should be as clean as possible.
You can now start embroidering. Remember that with cross-stitch the top stitches of the crosses must all slant in the same direction. If the stitches are correctly worked, those at the back should be parallel and not slanting. When threads on the wrong side are neatened, work with a sharp-pointed needle in the same direction as the stitches and tease out the thread if it is too thick.
To start with your cross-stitch, insert the needle and thread near the starting point, from the top down and bring the needle out to the top in the A-position (see diagram 3) of your cross-stitch. Insert it downwards at B and then again from C to the top and D to the bottom. While doing this, hold the end of the thread and later pull it towards the back to work it into the already embroidered stitches.
With a second thread you would already have stitches into which you could work the thread before you start.
Never work a dark thread into a lighter one (for example dark blue into pink) as it will show on the right side of the embroidery.
For the outline – a very important part of the finishing off of the picture – use ordinary back-stitch.
Embroider with one or two threads, unless otherwise specified. The back-stitch is worked horizontally, vertically, or slanted over one stitch on the right side of the fabric, and over two stitches on the wrong side (see diagram 4).

FRENCH KNOT

This stitch is often used as an eye, a spot or a flower.
Bring the thread to the front of the material where the knot is required. Hold the thread down with your left thumb. Now, insert the point of the needle from left to right behind the thread and twist it (three times in order to get a thick knot) from right to left around the needle while still holding the thread firmly. Insert the needle to the wrong side, close to where it came out, but do not let go of the thread before it has been completely pulled to the wrong side. The knots must be neatly sewn, otherwise the effect will be lost. (See diagram 5.)
When the article is completed, use a warm iron and a damp cloth to press it on the wrong side. Make sure that the ironing board is clean and well padded.
Should the embroidery be dirty, it can be carefully washed, because most modern threads are colourfast. Be careful with the fabric, however. Always test a piece before you wash the article. Some colours run and may therefore ruin a completed piece of work.
Use pure soap flakes and lukewarm water and soak the article for a while. Squeeze it carefully – do not rub – and then rinse. First use lukewarm and then cold water.
Place the article flat on a clean towel in order to dry and remember not to wring the fabric.

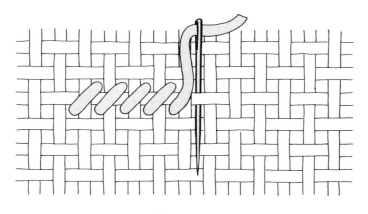

Diagram 1

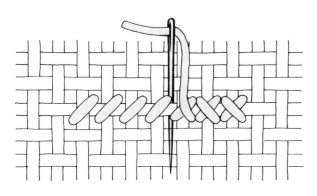

Diagram 2

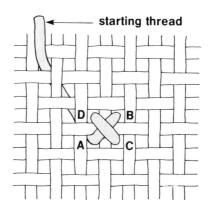

Diagram 3

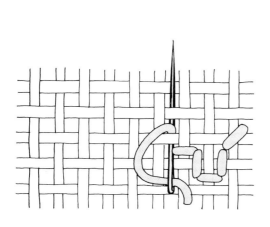

Diagram 4

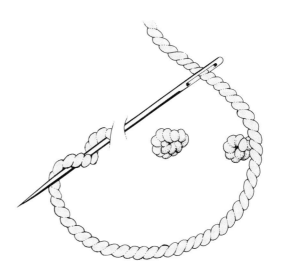

Diagram 5

Rabbit

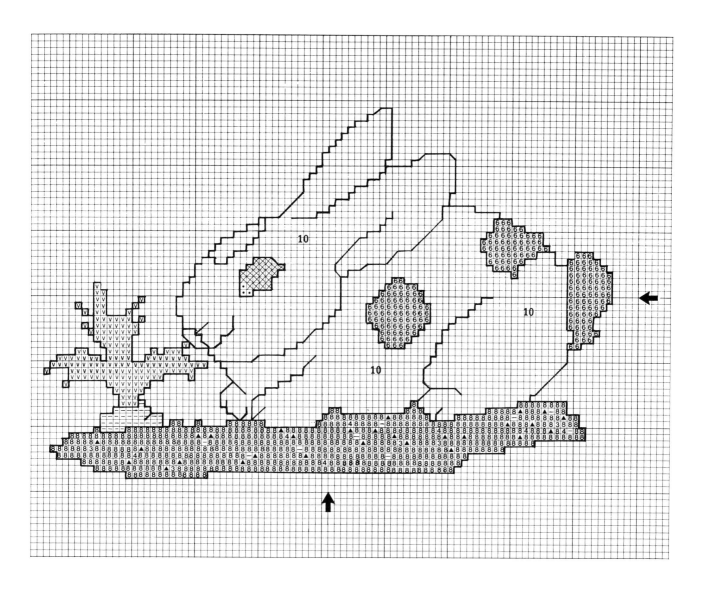

(width) 90 × 57 (height)

× – 838
• – blanc (white)
6 – 842
10 – 841 (2 strands) (the body of the rabbit)
8 – 3348
– – 922
v – 701
▲ – 702
3 – 743
4 – 793

Outline rabbit with two threads 838.
Outline grass and carrot with 3345.

(width) 80 × 43 (height)

⊠ – 793
■ – 310
6 – 3348
2 – 895
/ – 435
3 – 433
• – 834

Outline tiger with two threads 310.

Tiger

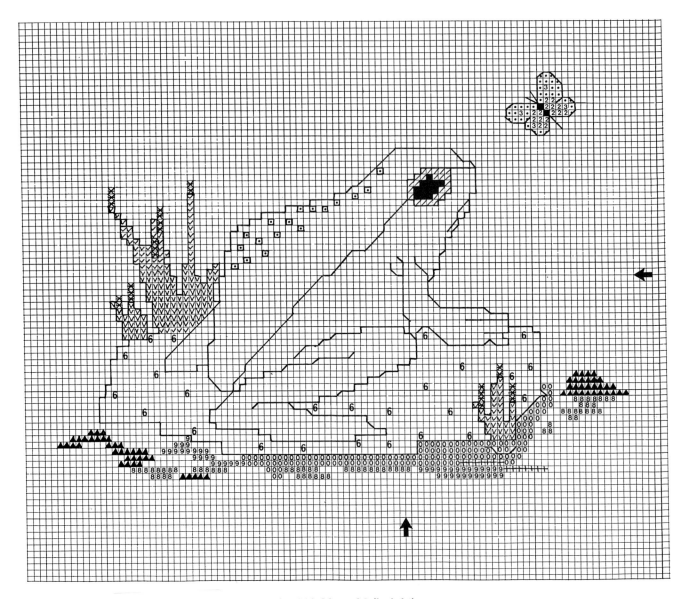

(width) 92 × 64 (height)

■ – 310 (black)
• – 745
2 – 783
/ – blanc (white)
3 – 518
6 – 841
▲ – 798
8 – 799
* – 919
○ – 807
v – 702

The body of the frog 3345

9 – 794
+ – 800
Outline frog with 310.
Outline rock with 839.
Outline grass with 890.

10

Frog

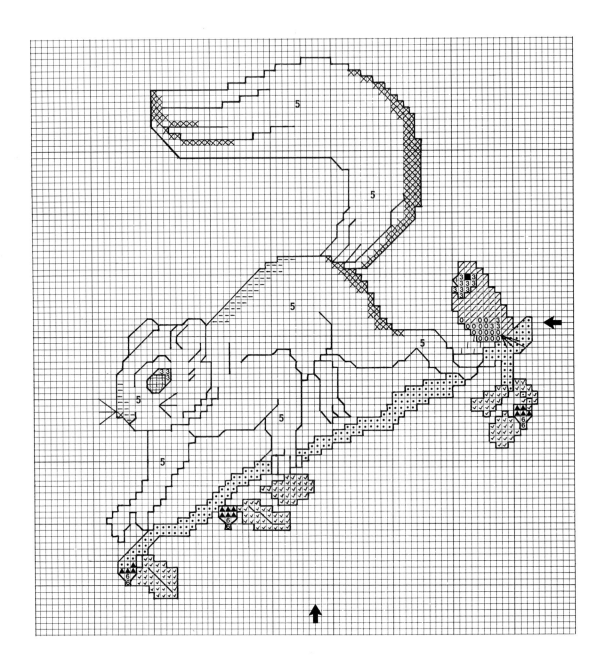

(width) 73 × 87 (height)

1 — 921
× — 839
— — 840
3 — blanc (white)
+ — 807
• — 833
6 — 722
v — 701
▲ — 301
/ — 798
■ — 820
○ — 958 (also the tail)
5 — 841 (2 strands)

Outline with 838 (2 threads).

Squirrel

Parrot

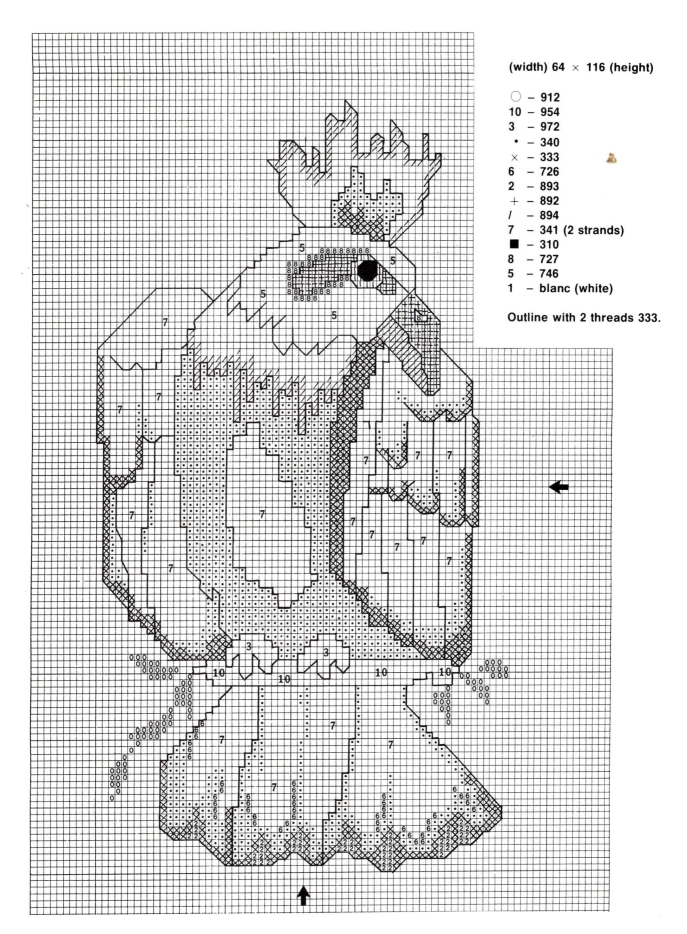

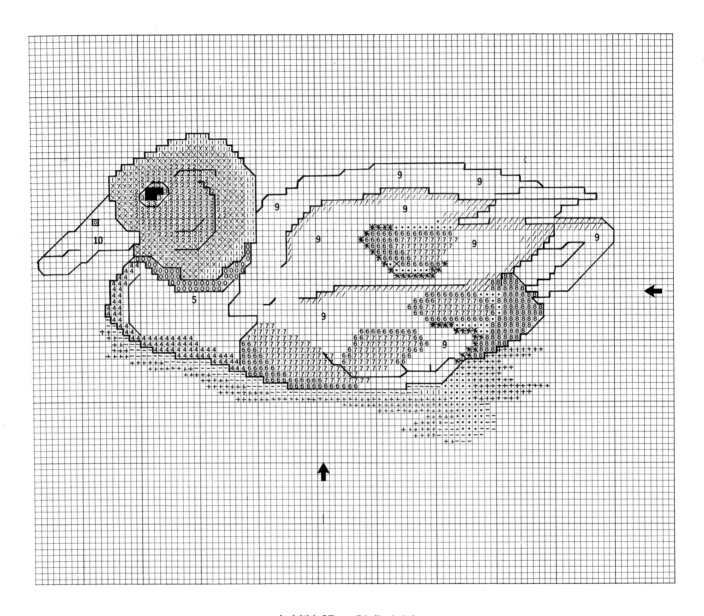

(width) 97 × 51 (height)

× — 986
■ — 310
1 — 895
2 — 989
3 — 433
4 — 434
5 — 3065
6 — 924
7 — 926
8 — 844
9 — 928 (2 strands)
10 — 834
— — 336
+ — 312
• — 435
* — 319
○ — blanc (white)

Outline with 2 threads 844.

Duck

(width) 82 × 104 (height)

- ■ – 310
- 2 – 844
- 6 – 645
- 7 – 646
- \ – 647
- 13 – 648
- 8 – 415 (2 strands)
- — – 948
- t – blanc (white)
- r – 797
- • – 958
- ○ – 3609
- v – 701
- + – 444
- 5 – 472
- s – 307
- / – 798
- 3 – 209
- × – 761
- : – 605

**Outline ostrich with 2 threads 310.
Easter egg with DMC golden thread (also the spots on the easter egg)
Grass patch with 319 (1 thread)**

Ostrich

(width) 105 × 70 (height)

× – 597
○ – 602
2 – 743
+ – 605
6 – 603
10 – 598
3 – 742
/ – 318
— – 317

**3 Threads 745 for the wings of the butterfly
Outline with 317.**

Butterfly

Tortoise

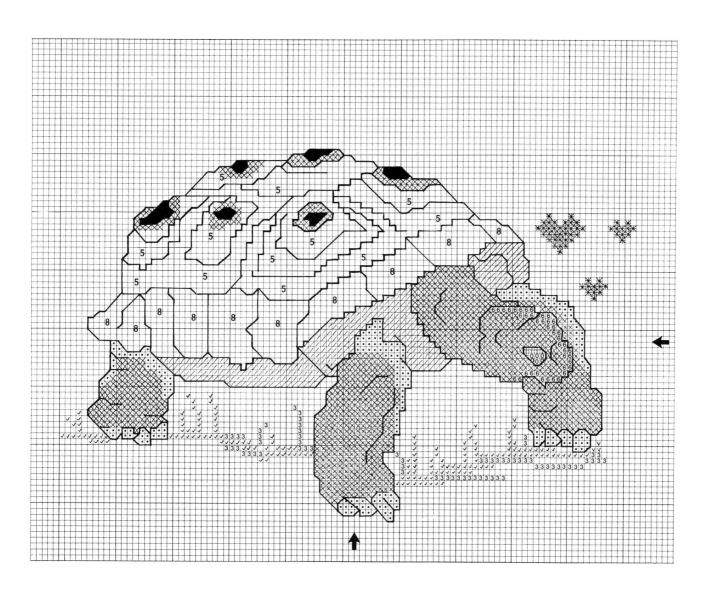

(width) 102 × 64 (height)

+ – blanc (white)
5 – 436
■ – 938
8 – 434
× – 801
• – 898
v – 561
3 – 954
6 – 437
* – 816
/ – 644
○ – 310

Outline tortoise with two threads 310.

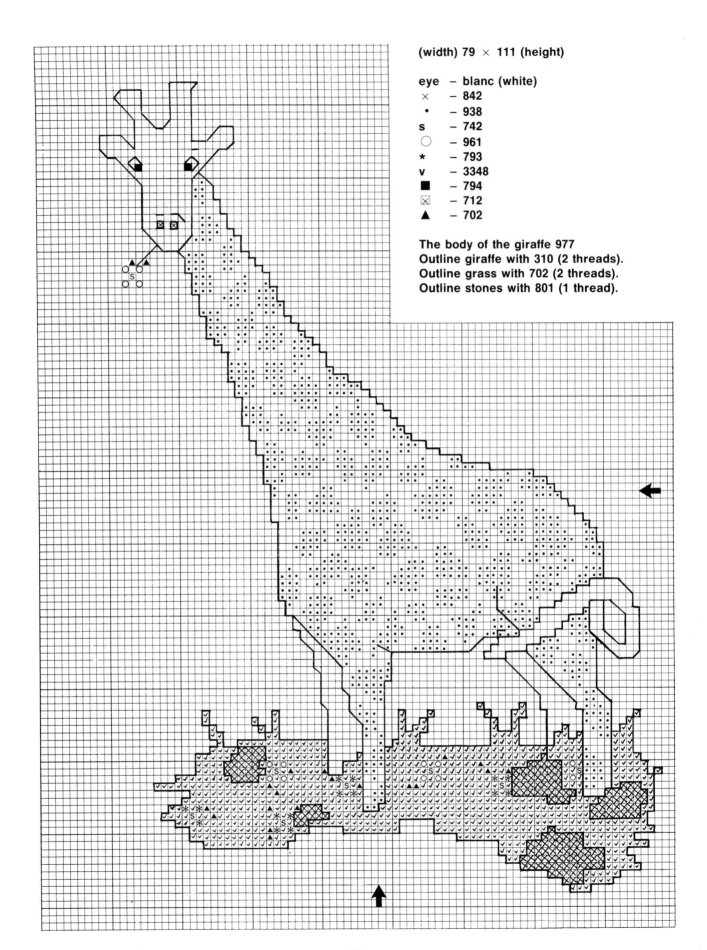

Giraffe

Zebra

(width) 91 × 104 (height)

E – 310
• – 932
× – 950
v – 912
3 – 561
8 – 975
6 – 817
▲ – 444

The body of the zebra blanc (white) 3 threads
Use 796 for the eye.
Outline with 310 (2 threads).

(width) 98 × 79 (height)

- • – 782
- + – 975
- * – 310 (black)
- 10 – 738
- 8 – 761
- ■ – 801
- 16 – 680
- // – 3347
- × – 775
- 9 – 780
- v – 989
- ▲ – 904
- 13 – blanc (white)
- 3 – 712
- ○ – 356
- / – 783
- – – 676

Outline with 2 threads 801.
Use French knots for the flowers 3018.

Lion

Hippopotamus

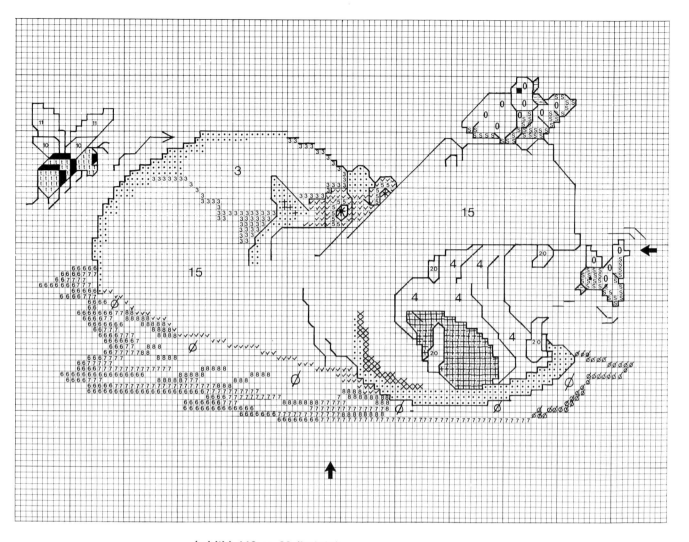

(width) 113 × 62 (height)

■ — 310
○ — 993
S — 992
— — 304
6 — 742
10 — 745
11 — 743
• — 413
× — 317
3 — 414
+ — 758
4 — 3064
5 — blanc (white)
20 — 712
* — 995
ø — 312
6 — 775
7 — 334
8 — 823
15 — 415 (3 threads)

Outline hippopotamus with 310 (2 threads).
Outline the bee and the little birds with 310 (1 thread).

(width) 89 × 68 (height)

- `+` – 761
- `10` – 712
- `/` – 951
- `○` – blanc (white)
- `×` – 950
- `6` – 414
- `5` – 415
- `■` – 368
- `3` – 3689
- `4` – 3688
- `8` – 3687
- `•` – 844

Outline with 1 thread 844.

Kittens